English
for
academic
study:

Reading

Course Book

John Slaght and Paddy Harben

University of
Reading

CALS
Centre for
Applied Language Studies

Garnet
EDUCATION

Credits

Published by
Garnet Publishing Ltd.
8 Southern Court
South Street
Reading RG1 4QS, UK

Copyright © 2009 University of Reading's
Centre for Applied Language Studies, The University of
Reading, and the authors.

First published 2004
Second edition published 2006
Reprinted 2008, 2010
Fully revised 2009

The right of John Slaght and Paddy Harben to be identified
as the authors of this work has been asserted in accordance
with the Copyright, Design and Patents Act 1988.

ISBN: 978 1 85964 484 3

British Cataloguing-in-Publication Data
A catalogue record for this book is available from
the British Library.

Production
Project manager: Simone Davies
Project consultant: Rod Webb
Editorial team: Penny Analytis, Emily Clarke,
                      Chris Gough, Fiona McGarry,
                      Nicky Platt
Art director: Mike Hinks
Design and layout: Nick Asher
Illustration: Mike Hinks, Doug Nash
Photography: Corbis: NASA, Warrick Page,
                      Radu Sigheti, Lee Snider;
                      Getty: Derek Belsey, Keith Brofsky,
                      Floresco Productions, John Foxx,
                      David Sanger, Shaul Schwartz,
                      Beowulf Sheehan, Rob & Ann
                      Simpson, Inti St Clair, Travel Ink
                      Mike Hinks;
                      The United Nations.

Every effort has been made to trace the copyright holders
and we apologize in advance for any unintentional
omission. We will be happy to insert the appropriate
acknowledgements in any subsequent editions.

Printed and bound in Lebanon by International Press:
interpress@int-press.com

The authors and publishers wish to acknowledge the
following use of material:

'Economics focus: On the move' © The Economist
Newspaper Limited, London (May 12th, 2001).

'Does Class Size Matter?' reprinted with permission.
Copyright © 2001 by *Scientific American*, Inc.
All rights reserved.

From Atkinson/Atkinson/SmithBem/Nolen-Hoeksema/
Harcourt, Inc.. Hilgard's Introduction to Psychology, 12E.
(c) 1996 Wadsworth, a part of Cengage Learning, Inc.
Reproduced by permission. www.cengage.com/permissions

Middleton, N., 'Acid rain in Norway' in *Geography
Review*, Vol. 11, No. 4. (1998) Reprinted with permission
© Philip Allan Updates.

Everett, M., 'Impact – Skylarks in decline' in *Biological
Sciences Review*, Vol. 10, No. 2. (1997) Reprinted with
permission © Philip Allan Updates.

'Statistics Without Tears: A Primer for Non-Mathematicians'
by Derek Rowntree (Penguin Books, 1982). Copyright ©
Derek Rowntree, 1982. Pages 14–21 reproduced by
permission of Penguin Books Ltd.

'Common Questions about Climate Change'
(pages 4–12), reprinted with permission © United
Nations Environment Programme and World
Meteorological Organization.

'The Global Village: Challenges for a Shrinking
Planet', reprinted with permission from *The Global
Village: Challenges for a Shrinking Planet* (*Understanding
Global Issues 98/7*).

'The New Linguistic Order' in *Foreign Policy*, Winter
1998–99 (pages 26–39), Joshua A. Fishman

Contents

Acknowledgements

The Reading course has been developed to dovetail with the Writing course produced by CALS colleague, Anne Pallant. Anne has played a major role in reviewing material at every stage of development and helping refine the rationale behind the reading into writing approach.

Further significant cooperation in reviewing and editing the materials has come from present and former colleagues at CALS, particularly Ros Richards, Joan McCormack, Colin Campbell, Paul Stocks, Heather Bagley and Sarah Brewer.

In the production of the pilot editions, Paul Thompson contributed considerable IT support and Jill Riley showed great patience and good humour in her painstaking editing and typing.

Pre-sessional teachers in 2000–2005 gave invaluable feedback during trialling of the texts, tasks and teacher's notes.

Many thanks to all the above and also to the many hundreds of students who have already worked with pilot editions of these materials.

A big apology to anyone I have omitted from this list.

John Slaght, Author, April 2009,
Centre for Applied Languages Studies,
University of Reading, UK

Reference to Source Book texts

Book map

Topic	Skills focus

1 • Economics focus: On the move

- Deciding if a text is useful: predicting content
- Word building from a text
- Identifying the organization of a text: analyzing a text to establish the purpose
- Writing a summary of part of the text: complete a gap-fill model
- Dealing with unknown vocabulary: identifying word classes and relative importance of lexis
- Evaluating the level of content: identifying writer's attitude from a range of options
- Reading for a purpose: identifying whether a text is suitable for the reader's purpose
- Reviewing reading styles: reflecting on activities of the unit

1 • The influence of class size on academic achievement

- Predicting text content: reflecting on personal experience
- Reading for a purpose: predicting content
- Reading selectively: identifying whether a text contains useful information
- Identifying the writer's purpose
- Understanding referencing in texts

• A case study: Shining star

- Reading a text for closer understanding (1): activities to encourage close reading

• The Asian paradox: Huge class sizes, high scores

- Reading a text for closer understanding (2): activities to promote close reading
- Thinking critically about the text: reflect on outcome of reading the three texts
- Making use of the text: complete a written assignment

2 • Interaction between nature and nurture

- Accessing background knowledge: predicting content based on personal experience
- Vocabulary development
- Reading for general understanding: skim read to answer global questions
- Developing further understanding
- Understanding the main argument: identify the best summary
- Note-taking from the text: summarizing specific aspects of the text
- Developing understanding of the text: understanding sequences of events
- Working with words from the text: classify words and discuss their relationships

• Capacities of the newborn

- Pre-reading discussion
- Inferring meaning from the text
- Summarizing information from the text (1)
- Summarizing information from the text (2)

• Hearing, taste and smell

- Using background knowledge
- Reading for a purpose and creating a summary

3 • Acid rain in Norway

- Raising text awareness: activities to elicit personal experience of topic
- Taking information from displayed information: using headings, illustrations, etc.
- Writing a global summary: compare individual work with model summary

• Skylarks in decline

- More global summary practice: compare individual work with model summary

Topic	Skills focus
4 Making sense of experience	Statistics in practice: awareness raising about the topic
	Identifying main and supporting points: read and compare answers
	Continuing to identify main and minor points: read and compare answers
	Summarizing key points (1): complete a gap-fill model
	Summarizing key points (2): complete a gap-fill model
What is statistics?	Concentrating on the main points: read and write main points
Descriptive and inferential statistics	Note-taking practice: take notes or annotate text in preparation for writing
	Recalling information from the text: write a short summary
5 Extra-textual information	Overviewing the text: using extra-textual information and the text introduction
Common questions about climate change	Writing into reading: compare own notes with information from the text
	Identifying topic sentences
	Understanding the general meaning of a text: develop understanding of text organization as a means of extracting an overview
	Topic sentences and supporting sentences: read and identify main points and supporting details
	Recalling the text: summarize in writing
Are human activities contributing to climate change?	Identifying relevant information in a text: find key points and evaluate relevance of text
	Detailed reading: read and complete a summary
	Recalling the text from memory: write notes from memory
What human activities contribute to climate change	Making use of figures and tables: relate display information to sections of the text
	Reading displayed information: relate display information to sections
	Inferring meaning from a text: infer meaning and include in a summary
	Making use of a text: prepare oral presentation or written assignment
6 Introduction	• Pre-reading discussion
	• Checking predictions
The shrinking planet	• Thinking about the topic
	• Recalling the text from memory
	• Checking the text for details
	• Making use of the text content
	• Reading for a purpose
Economic globalization	• Asking questions about the text
	• Identifying key information in the text
	• Preparing to complete the Focus task
Community & conflict	• Thinking about the topic
The sharing of sovereignty	• Developing understanding of the text
Converging or diverging?	• Identifying relevant information for the Focus task
	• Completing an assignment
7 The new linguistic order	• Deciding how to read a text
	• Reading an introductory case study
	• Understanding subject-specific vocabulary
	• Predicting content to help understanding
	• Selecting relevant information from the text
	• Fulfilling your reading purpose

Introduction

In this course you will be working on four main aspects of academic reading:
- reading for a specific academic purpose;
- working on effective reading strategies;
- detailed comprehension of sentences and paragraphs;
- text analysis.

1. Reading for a specific academic purpose

Here you will be concentrating on getting information from the text which will help you complete an academic task. For example, you may need to:

- complete an assignment on a specific question, for which it is necessary to combine information from various sources;

- get an introductory overview of a new topic in order to assist with listening to a series of lectures on that topic;

- add new knowledge about a topic to what you already know. This could be, for example, note-taking for future exam revision or simply reading a text and thinking about what you have read in order to understand the topic better.

2. Working on effective reading strategies

The main strategies we will be looking at are:

- **Skimming**

  This involves **looking at a text quickly** in order to do one or more of the following:

  - Identify what the text is about (the topic)

  - Identify the main idea of the text

  - Decide how useful the text is for your purposes

  - Decide how you will make use of the text

  Skimming a text might involve looking at some or all of the following features of the text:

  - Title

  - Section headings

  - Abstract or summary provided by the writer

  - First and last paragraphs

  - First and last sentences of intervening paragraphs

  - Topic sentences in each paragraph (see also Glossary: paragraph leaders)

  Another form of skimming is when you are previewing a book in order to decide how useful it is for your purposes. In this situation, you might also look at one or more of the following:

  - Information about the author and/or publication details

  - Contents page

  - Foreword and/or Introduction

  - Index

- **Predicting**

   Predicting means using what you already know about the topic, what you want to learn about the topic from the text, and what you have learnt from your previewing in order to **guess what kind of information the text will contain and how useful it will be**. You will often be surprised how much you already know about a text before you even begin reading. Brainstorming your prior knowledge will help you to understand the text.

- **Scanning**

   Scanning involves **finding words** (or other symbols, such as figures) which have particular importance for you. When you are scanning, you already know the form of the words or symbols you are looking for. When you scan, you normally focus on small parts of the text only.

- **Search reading**

   Search reading means quickly **finding ideas** which are particularly important for you. This is different from scanning, because you don't know the exact words you are looking for in advance and cannot make a direct match.

- **Identifying the main ideas**

   This involves **understanding the writer's main points**. It may be possible to do this quite quickly after skimming the text. However, with more difficult texts it may only be possible to identify the main ideas after more detailed reading.

- **Careful reading**

   This involves **reading slowly and carefully** so that you understand every word in the text (or the part of the text that you are most interested in). You might do this in order to understand the details of the text and also to infer meaning that has not been directly stated (see below).

- **Inferring**

   Inferring means **obtaining meaning from the text that the writer has not explicitly stated**. Sometimes the writer expects you to fill in gaps in the text in order for it to make sense. Sometimes you may wish to infer why the author wrote the text, i.e., the writer's purpose, and also the writer's attitude to what s/he is writing about.

- **Dealing with unfamiliar words**

   When you find a word you don't understand in a text, you need to **decide first whether it is really necessary to understand the word**. Perhaps you can understand enough of the text without understanding the word, in which case you can ignore it. Alternatively, the context in which the word is located may allow you to guess the meaning of the word well enough to continue reading. If neither of these applies, you may have to look up the word in a dictionary. If you find you are using a dictionary so much that you are prevented from reading the text at a reasonable speed, the text may be too specialized for you, and you should consider finding another one which deals with the same topic in a more generalized way.

   An approach to dealing with new vocabulary is to decide whether you:

   - *need to know the word now to help you understand the text and use it later under different circumstances*. In this case, you will need some way of recording the word, e.g., in a vocabulary notebook. You will also have to decide whether to rely on working out the meaning of the word from context, or whether you need to check in a dictionary;

   - *only need to know the word now to help you understand the text*. This is often the case with technical words or low-frequency words. These are words which are not often used in English, even by native speakers of the language, except for specialist reasons. Of course, if you are reading a text in your academic area, you will need to know certain specialist vocabulary. You will need to record this vocabulary as well as use it so it becomes part of your active vocabulary, i.e., words that you use to communicate effectively;

- *don't need to know this word either now or in the future*. If the word does not prevent you from understanding the rest of the text, you probably do not need to worry about it. If the word occurs several times, however, you may feel it is necessary to work out its meaning or look it up and record it.

3. Detailed comprehension of sentences and paragraphs

In an academic context, much of your reading work will involve dealing with complete texts and extracting information from them in various ways, i.e., reading purposefully in order to make use of content. However, in order to fulfil your reading purpose, you may sometimes find it necessary to have a very precise understanding of specific sentences and paragraphs. There may be obstacles to your understanding in terms of grammar or ideas, or the text's organization or a combination of these. This is one area the course will help to solve.

Detailed comprehension involves analyzing the relationship between ideas within a specific sentence or between a sequence of sentences of up to paragraph length – or even beyond. This precise knowledge might be required, for example, to infer meaning, to view the content critically, to enhance overall understanding or to formulate precise understanding.

4. Text analysis

It is often helpful to understand the way a text is organized in order to make the best use of it. The organization of a text can be considered at the global level; for example, the way that the text is organized into sections and paragraphs according to the purpose of the text and the type of text. In a report of an experiment, for example, it is very common to see the following pattern of organization:

- Title
- Abstract
- Introduction/background
- Method
- Results
- Conclusions
- References/bibliography

Another aspect of organization that can be useful to examine is how information is organized logically at the local level, i.e., within complex sentences or paragraphs.

As you can see, there are many different aspects of academic reading that we will be considering during the course. Whilst it is important to be aware of all these different aspects, it is also important to:

- **develop a flexible reading style**. Becoming a better academic reader is not just about mastering different aspects of reading. It is also important to decide which is the best way to read a text depending on the particular academic purpose that you have for reading it;

- **remember that the more you read, the better you will read**. Regular independent reading outside the classroom is essential for any student wishing to develop reading abilities such as fluency, greater reading speed, vocabulary acquisition and the strategies associated with successful reading.

You can improve your academic reading level by making decisions about:

- **why** you are reading;
- **what** you are reading;
- **how** you are reading;
- **how well** you are reading.

Task introduction

This unit will help you:
- practice and review the reading strategies outlined in the introduction;
- develop strategies for deciding if a text is useful;
- build vocabulary through reading;
- identify a text's organization;
- write a summary as part of understanding key issues.

The topic of this unit is based on an article about international migration and the integration of labour markets.

Text i-1 | Economics focus: On the move (Source Book pp. 5–6)

Focus task

Imagine you are going to attend an Economic History lecture about the link between migration and economic forces. This is a new subject for you, and you want to have some background information before attending your first lecture.

You have a number of articles on the subject, but you don't have time to read them all. You must therefore decide which ones to read. Text i-1 is an introduction to one of the articles. You have to decide whether the whole article would be useful. We will go through the stages that will help you make that decision.

Task 1: Deciding if a text is useful

1.1 **Read the paragraph in italics in Text i-1 (the introduction) in the Source Book. Who is the intended reader?**

a) a business analyst

b) an educated general reader

c) an Economics student

d) a historian

Write down one reason for your choice.

_____

_____

1.2 **Reread the paragraph in italics. What can you guess about the text content and the way it will be organized? Write down as many ideas as you can.**

_____

_____

_____

_____

1.3 Read Text i-1 and highlight any sections which are similar to the ideas you predicted.

Don't worry too much about difficult vocabulary at this stage, as you are reading for overall understanding. You will deal with some of the new vocabulary in Task 2. You will also be able to further check your predictions in the tasks that follow.

Task 2: Word building from a text

2.1 Find the word *immigration* in the subtitle of Text i-1. Scan the text to find other examples of this word. Note the line number and highlight any words that are connected.

2.2 Look for similar words such as *migration* (line 5). Use the three different forms of the word *immigration* you find to complete the table below.

Word used	Line number	Word class	Connected language
migration	line 18	noun	to restrict migration

2.3 Look at Ex 2.2 again. What verbs or adjectives could you form from the words you have used to complete the table? Write sentences to show how verbs or adjectives can be formed from the words in the table.

to migrate; people first migrated to America in the 17th century

Task 3: Identifying the organization of a text

3.1 Look at Text i-1. How is it divided? Where does this division occur? Discuss with a partner and then check with your teacher.

3.2 Look at the first part of the text (lines 1–98) and answer the questions. Discuss with your partner and then check with your teacher.

a) What is the main aim of paragraph 1?

The main aim is

b) What is the main purpose of paragraphs 2–4?

The purpose is

3.3 Look at the second part of the text. What is the main purpose of this part?

Highlight some words, phrases or even sentences in the text to support what you think is the main purpose of this second part.

The main purpose of the second part of the text is

3.4 Discuss with a partner and then check with your teacher.

Task 4: Writing a summary of part of the text

4.1 Reread the first part of Text i-1 (up to line 98) in the Source Book. As you read, underline any ideas that now seem clearer to you.

4.2 Now complete the summary below. Use one, two or three words in the gaps.

> There is a clear link between the history of migration to America and *economic factors*.
> At first, migration to America was very expensive and migrants were usually
> _____ or indentured labourers. However, as travel became easier,
> many more people _____ . This continued throughout
> _____ and early 20th century, but then war and
> _____ slowed down and even reversed migratory trends.
> After the Second World War, _____ increased again.

4.3 Reread the second part of the text. As you read, underline any ideas that now seem clearer to you.

4.4 **Now label the paragraphs A–E starting at line 100. Then match the summaries 1–3 to three of the paragraphs.**

1 ☐ Countries all over the world have experienced economic growth, and this factor is likely to encourage another wave of migration.

2 ☐ Countries with the greatest wealth are now in a position to be selective in the type of immigrant they want. This is good for these countries, but causes greater problems for the poorest, least-skilled migrants.

3 ☐ Both the immigrants involved and the countries where they migrate to can benefit from the migration of labour. However, at first, the workforce in these countries tends to suffer.

Task 5: Dealing with unknown vocabulary

This activity will help you practise the technique for dealing with unknown vocabulary described earlier in the unit. You may wish to reread the notes on page 10 before doing the task.

5.1 **All the following words and phrases appear in Text i-1. Which ones do you know already?**

makes plain (line 25); *harsh* (line 36); *indentured* (line 43); *slavery* (line 49); *falling* (line 65); *comparatively* (line 75–76); *net* (line 79); *feasible* (line 91); *expansionary* (line 124)

5.2 **Find the words in Ex 5.1 in the text and decide whether a, b or c applies.**

a) you need to know the word now and, if you don't already know it, add it to your active vocabulary;

b) you only need to know this word now because it would prevent you from understanding the general meaning of the text;

c) you don't need to know this word or, if you don't already know it, add it to your active vocabulary.

> **Study tip**
>
> All words belong to a particular word class, such as *noun, verb* or *adjective*. This is sometimes referred to as a *part of speech*. Identifying word class can help you work out the meaning of a particular word.

Complete the table by placing a tick (✓) in either column a, b or c.

Vocabulary	a	b	c	Word class
makes plain				
harsh				
indentured				
slavery				
falling				
comparatively				
net				
feasible				
expansionary				

5.3 Look at the following extract from the text. Write the word class of the underlined words. Use the following abbreviations: n = noun; vb = verb; pron = pronoun; adj = adjective; adv = adverb.

> The _world_ (n) _has experienced_ (vb) a _new_ (adj) era of _globalization_ (—),
> _which_ (—) _is_ (—) _much_ (—) _quicker_ (—).

5.4 Now complete the final column of the table in Ex 5.2 by filling in the word class.

Carry out this task by finding the words in the text and working out the word class from their position in relation to other words and their function in the text.

Task 6: Evaluating the level of content

When deciding on the value of a text for your academic reading purpose, it is often useful to think about the writer's attitude to the topic and his or her purpose for writing it.

6.1 What do you think was the writer's attitude and purpose when writing Text i-1? Discuss with a partner.

6.2 Bearing in mind your discussion in Ex 6.1, decide which of the following you most agree with.

a) to inform the reader about the topic

b) to persuade the reader to accept his or her opinion

c) to challenge ideas about the topic

d) to give a balanced opinion about the topic

e) to do all of these things

f) to do some of these things

6.3 Write down your conclusions about the writer's attitude and purpose.

My views on the writer's attitude and purpose:

Task 7: Reading for a purpose

7.1 Discuss the tasks you have done in this unit with a partner. Then decide whether you feel Text i-1 is suitable or not for your reading purpose, i.e., to get some background information before attending a lecture on migration and economic forces.

7.2 Summarize your answer in one sentence.

Task 8: Reviewing reading styles

8.1 In small groups or with a partner, discuss the following questions to help you reflect on the activities you have carried out in this unit.

a) Why is it useful to predict the contents of a text before reading it?

b) What are reading strategies? How can they help the reader?

c) What is global understanding of a text? Why is it useful to get a global understanding of a text?

d) Why is reading very slowly through a text word by word often an unsuccessful reading strategy?

e) Why is it often important to read only parts of a text?

f) Why is it useful to consider who the intended reader is before starting to read a text?

8.2 With the whole class or in small groups, discuss the suggested answers that your teacher will give you. Make a note of important ideas below.

Academic achievement

This unit will help you:
- use your prior knowledge to help you understand what you are reading;
- practise reading for a specific purpose;
- make decisions about the relevance of a text in terms of reading purpose;
- read selectively in order to use appropriate information from the text.

The topic of this unit concerns factors which may lead to improvement in academic performance among students. It is based on three major research projects carried out in the United States.

Text 1-1 The influence of class size on academic achievement (Source Book pp. 7–9)

Task 1: Predicting text content

1.1 Think about what factors can have an influence on the academic achievement of the students in a school, college or university.

1.2 Look at the following list of possible influences and rate the ideas on a scale of 1–5 (1 = *very little influence*, 5 = *very strong influence*).

Influence on academic performance	Rating
Resources available (e.g., computers, laboratories, textbooks)	
Teacher level (qualifications, experience, etc.)	
Student motivation	

1.3 Add and rate some of your own ideas. Then compare your list and ratings with a partner.

Focus task

Your reason for reading Text 1-1 is to get some background information to help you write the following essay.

What are the aims of academic study and how can they be achieved?

Task 2: Reading for a purpose

2.1 Look carefully at the title of Text 1-1 in the Source Book. Do you think that the text will be useful for writing an assignment about academic achievement? Share your conclusions with another student.

2.2 Read the introduction to Text 1-1 (lines 1–66). As you read, try to make up your mind about how useful this text might be for your purpose. When you have finished reading, circle and complete the following sentence.

The text may / will / will not be useful because _____

_____

_____

_____

Task 3: Reading selectively

3.1 Read the subheading (lines 67–68) and think about your own opinion on the issue. Do you think that smaller class sizes help to improve academic performance? Circle your answer then write one reason for your choice below.

Yes / No / Not sure

_____

_____

_____

3.2 Below are some notes that have been made by another student on Text 1-1. Read lines 67–117 and tick the points mentioned in the text.

a) ☐ *easier to concentrate*

b) ☐ *students prefer smaller classes*

c) ☐ *more cooperative learning occurs*

d) ☐ *more help for students with problems*

e) ☐ *students develop good methods of learning*

f) ☐ *more opportunities to use resources if fewer students in class*

g) ☐ *students get much better academic results*

3.3 Read lines 69–72. What does *anecdotal* mean? Try to guess the meaning of this word by looking carefully at the whole sentence.

If the ideas in this paragraph are *anecdotal*, think about how seriously you should take them into account when writing your assignment.

3.4 Read lines 97–117 and underline specific information from this paragraph which you might use to help in the completion of the Focus task.

Think about:

- how useful you think this paragraph might be in relation to the Focus task;
- whether you think the sources are reliable.

3.5 With a partner, compare and justify your choice of information for all four questions.

Task 4: Identifying the writer's purpose

4.1 Read lines 118–192 and decide on the main functions of this section of text from the choices given below. For each choice, rate the function from 0–5 depending on how sure you are (5 = very sure).

Study tip

It can be very helpful to recognize why the writer has written a text, or a section of a text, i.e., what the function of the text is.

Function	Rating
a) To persuade the readers to accept a certain point of view.	
b) To explain the importance of using research data instead of *anecdotal* explanations.	
c) To evaluate the importance of the research carried out into the effect of classroom size on academic achievement.	
d) To describe the research method used in various parts of the US into the effect of classroom size on academic achievement.	

4.2 What is the function (or functions) of Figure 1: *Milestone studies in class size* (Source Book page 9)?

a) to summarize the content of the text

b) to outline the content of certain relevant research

c) to explain the importance of the STAR project

d) to compare the data from research about class size

Task 5: Understanding referencing in texts

Referencing in a text is a way of linking words and ideas together, thus making the text more cohesive and easier to understand. The following activity will provide practice in this important skill.

Study tip

An effective reader makes use of referencing in a text to gain a clear understanding of what the author wishes to convey.

5.1 Look at line 119 of Text 1-1. What information or idea in the text do the words *these findings* refer to?

a) The US Department of Education

b) The National Assessment of Educational Progress

c) Project STAR

5.2   What other words or phrases (lines 119–148) refer to the same data?

a) _____ (line number _____)

b) _____ (line number _____)

5.3   What reasons do the writers give for ignoring the data? Complete the list below, using a similar note form.

a) Decreased dropout rates _____

b) _____

c) _____

d) _____

e) More experienced teachers _____

5.4   What factors, according to the writers, made Project STAR better than other *poorly designed* studies? Complete the list below, using a similar note form.

a) _____

b) The research was carried out over a number of years _____

c) _____

d) _____

e) No new curricular methods _____

Text 1-2 A case study: Shining star (Source Book p. 10)

Task 6: Reading a text for closer understanding (1)

6.1   What general point is made in the first paragraph of Text 1-2 (lines 1–11)? Find a short phrase which best summarizes this conclusion.

_____

_____

_____

6.2 In the second paragraph, which of the following benefits of smaller classes do Finn and Achilles (1990) identify in their review of the project? Answer *true* or *false* and add the line number from where you found the answer.

a) Better academic performance in small-sized classes. _____ (line number _____)

b) Students benefit at an early stage in small classes. _____ (line number _____)

c) Students later continue to perform well in normal-sized classes. _____ (line number _____)

d) Average students make the most progress. _____ (line number _____)

e) Minority groups gained the most significant benefits. _____ (line number _____)

f) On average, ethnic minority students improved by one-fifth of standard deviation. _____ (line number _____)

6.3 In the final paragraph, which of the findings of Finn and Achilles (ibid.) in Ex 6.2 does Hanushek comment on? Put a tick (✓) when Hanushek agrees and a cross (✗) when he disagrees. Write *N/A* if Hanushek does not mention these findings.

a) _____

b) _____

c) _____

d) _____

e) _____

f) _____

6.4 To what extent do you feel that the analyses of Project STAR will help you with the Focus task? Rate your opinion 0–5 (0 = not at all). Discuss your answer with a partner.

Text 1-3 The Asian paradox: Huge classes, high scores (Source Book p. 11)

Task 7: Reading a text for closer understanding (2)

7.1 Discuss with a partner or in groups what you know about academic performance in developed Asian countries, and how academic success is achieved.

7.2 Read lines 1–65 of Text 1-3. As you read, remember to highlight ideas which might be useful for the Focus task.

7.3 What is your understanding of the 'Asian paradox'?
What one word in the text (lines 17–35) gives a reason for this Asian paradox?

_____

7.4 Find other short phrases in the rest of the paragraph (lines 35–48) which might provide further reasons for the apparent academic success of Japanese students.

_____

_____

_____

_____

_____

_____

_____

7.5 Having read the text, have you found any information that might be useful for the Focus task?

Task 8: Thinking critically about the text

8.1 Look at the list of possible influences on academic performance in Task 1 (page 18). Are there any new influences you would like to add to the table, and any which you wish to delete?

Influence on academic performance	Rating

8.2 If you added any influences to your table, what rating would you give them, on a scale of 1–5?

Task 9: Making use of the text

You now have some information that may help with the Focus task which you will be given in order to complete Unit 1 of _English for academic study: Writing_, if you are studying that course.

Decide now if, and how, you can use the information in Texts 1-1, 1-2 and 1-?

Unit summary

In this unit you have thought about using your prior knowledge to help you understand what you are reading and made decisions about the relevance of a text in terms of reading purpose. You have learnt to identify the writer's purpose and to read selectively in order to use appropriate information from the text.

1 **Complete this summary about the reading skills you practised in the first unit with some of the words from the box.**

> understanding   expertly   prior   title   critically   predictions
> meaning   subheadings   selectively   purpose

It is easier to read a text if you have some _____ knowledge of the topic that the text is about. This will help you to make _____ and will give you a _____, which you always need when you read. Knowing why you are reading and what you are looking for will help you to both enjoy a text and focus on it better. Reading the _____ and any _____ there might be will help you to quickly know if you want to read a text and how useful it will be to you. It is important to read _____, especially if you are short of time. Some parts of a text will provide the information you need while other parts will be less important. You will usually read a text quickly first to get a general idea of what it is about and then read more carefully for closer _____ and to be able to think _____ about the content.

2 **Look at these possible topics of a reading passage. How much prior knowledge do you have of each topic? Mark each topic as follows:**

L – I know a lot about this topic so I could make plenty of predictions.

S – I know something about this topic and so I could make a few predictions.

N – I know very little or nothing about this topic so I wouldn't be able to make any predictions.

a)   increasing traffic congestion in major cities

b)   special education for children with learning difficulties

c)   the growth in the popularity of baseball in Asian countries

d)   the intelligence of dolphins

e)   the origins of development of paper making

> For web resources relevant to this unit, see:
>
> **www.englishforacademicstudy.com/student/reading/links**
>
> These weblinks will provide you with comprehensive information on the micro-skills of reading and the differences between conventional and academic reading.

2 Early human development

This unit will help you:
- read about human development, focusing on the relationship between *nature* and *nurture*;
- learn how to make use of the knowledge you already have about a topic before you read more;
- recognize key words and find out the meaning of difficult/unfamiliar words;
- quickly identify the main points of the text that you are reading;
- read parts of a text more carefully in order to make use of it fully according to your purpose;
- practise summarizing useful information that you have found in a text.

The topic of this unit concerns human development at an early age, focusing on the relationship between *nature* and *nurture*.

Text 2-1 | Interaction between nature and nurture (Source Book pp. 12–13)

Task 1: Accessing background knowledge

1.1 **The following is the first sentence of a text about nature and nurture. Think about the information it contains and how it is connected with the picture. Then tick which of a–d best represents what you know about this topic.**

> The question of whether heredity ('nature') or environment ('nurture') is more important in determining the course of human development has been debated through the centuries.

Atkinson, R. L. *et al, Hilgard's Introduction to Psychology*, 13th edition (1999). © 1996.

a) ☐ Nothing

b) ☐ A little

c) ☐ Quite a lot

d) ☐ A lot

1.2 **Tick the statement that you think is most important in determining the course of human development.**

a) ☐ Nature (genes) is the most important.

b) ☐ Nurture (the environment you live in) is the most important.

c) ☐ Nature and nurture are equally important.

d) ☐ I'm not sure.

Task 2: Vocabulary development

2.1 **The lexical items a–t all occur in Text 2-1 in the Source Book. Match with the definitions 1–20. Write the appropriate numbers in the boxes supplied. Use a dictionary when necessary.**

a) nature	**1**	☐	a baby before it is born
b) nurture	**2**	☐	the effect of one thing on another
c) senses	**3**	☐	an infectious illness
d) malleable	**4**	☐	egg
e) heredity	**5**	☐	to get faster
f) personality traits	**6**	☐	inborn, already present at the time of birth
g) environment	**7**	☐	inheriting characteristics from previous generations
h) genetic	**8**	☐	natural processes
i) innate	**9**	☐	permanent characteristics of somebody's behaviour
j) biological	**10**	☐	processes caused by surroundings
k) ovum	**11**	☐	related to brain processes
l) fetus	**12**	☐	related to language, especially when it is spoken
m) German measles	**13**	☐	related to the mother
n) maternal	**14**	☐	relating to the information that is coded in the cells of the body
o) interaction	**15**	☐	to repeat a skill to improve it
p) to practise	**16**	☐	sight, taste, touch, etc.
q) to accelerate	**17**	☐	surroundings
r) neurological	**18**	☐	to bring up or educate (children)
s) to rear	**19**	☐	to do with the physical processes of living things
t) verbal	**20**	☐	very flexible and changeable

2.2 **The following two lexical items are defined in the text. Find them and write an appropriate definition for each.**

maturation (Paragraph D)

_____

_____

motor behaviours (Paragraph F)

_____

_____

Task 3: Reading for general understanding

Read through Text 2-1 to get a general idea about its contents. As you read, think about your answers to Task 1.

a) Does the text confirm or contradict your answer to Ex 1.2?

b) According to the text, which is a more powerful influence on the development of a child, nature or nurture?

Task 4: Developing further understanding

4.1 Read Paragraphs A–C of Text 2-1. Which of the people in the box are connected with the following ideas? Some ideas may relate to more than one of them.

> John Locke   modern psychologists   Darwin   Skinner & Watson

a) A scientific explanation which supported the view that nature was more important than nurture in human development.

b) Human development is determined entirely by experience.

c) Human development can be easily influenced or changed.

d) Both hereditary and environmental factors are important in human development.

4.2 Read Paragraphs D–H of Text 2-1. Which paragraph discusses the following ideas?

a) The unchanging stages in the learning of motor skills.

b) Nature's role in shaping certain basic physical features.

c) The development of language skills.

d) The effect of environmental factors such as illness, or the habits of the mother on natural human development.

e) The effects of training on motor skills.

Task 5: Understanding the main argument

Read the following sentences and tick the one that summarizes the main argument most accurately.

a) ☐ Most experts today agree that babies mainly develop as a result of the environment in which they live, and that the type of adult they become is determined by the early training they are given.

b) ☐ According to current opinion, a combination of natural development before and after birth, and the experiences which infants have, influence their processes of maturation.

c) ☐ Today, scientists believe that humans evolve into their final adult form as the result of biological processes which alone determine the development of motor skills and the ability to speak.

d) ☐ There have been many debates about the main influences on early human development throughout history, and even now, many scientists are unable to agree about this issue.

Task 6: Note-taking from the text

Imagine you are writing an essay about early human development. You have decided to include a table that summarizes the ways in which early human development can be influenced by nature and nurture.

Complete the table below, referring back to Text 2-1 as necessary.

Table 1: *The influence of nature and nurture on early human development*

Influences of *nature* on early human development	Influences of *nurture* on early human development
Genetic structure of fertilized ovum determines sex of fetus, colour of hair, general body size, etc.	Abnormal uterine environment can affect maturation process, e.g., if mother contracts German measles.

Source: *Hilgard's Introduction to Psychology*, 12th edition by Atkinson. ©1996. pp 70-71.

Task 7: Developing understanding of the text

Read Text 2-1 again and choose the time periods from the box which correspond to the ideas below. Some ideas may relate to more than one time period.

17th century   19th century   1930s   second half of 20th century   20th century

a) Children's development can be completely shaped by training.

_____

b) If children are given practical encouragement, they will learn to walk more quickly.

_____

c) Human development only occurs after birth.

_____

d) The hereditary view supports the biological theory.

_____

e) Encouragement from people can speed up children's development of speech.

_____

f) Children have inherited characteristics which develop naturally after birth, but are not influenced by the environment.

_____

g) Environmental factors can affect human development before birth.

_____

Task 8: Working with words from the text

8.1 **Sort the words in the box below into word groups, e.g., parts of speech, similar meanings, etc.**
You may decide you need a number of different groups, and some words may come into more than one group.

> to accelerate   biological   environment   fetus   genetic
> German measles   heredity   innate   interaction   malleable
> maternal   nature   neurological   nurture   ovum
> personality   traits   to practise   to rear   senses   verbal

8.2 **Explain your word groups to a partner and establish which words do not seem to fit into any of the groups?**

Text 2-2 | Capacities of the newborn (Source Book p. 14)

This section concerns the capacities of newborn babies, still within the overall topic of early human development. There is a focus on search reading and summarizing useful information found in the text.

Task 9: Pre-reading discussion

In your opinion, how well prepared are newborn babies to learn from their environment? Which of the following do you think is most likely? Discuss your answer with your group.

a) They are poorly prepared and are totally confused by what is going on around them.

b) They are well prepared and are ready to learn quickly.

Task 10: Inferring meaning from the text

Read Paragraph A of Text 2-2 and answer the following questions.

a) What are the *sensory systems* (line 7) mentioned by the writer?

b) What is the writer's answer to the question in Task 9?

Task 11: Summarizing information from the text (1)

11.1 **Without reference to the text, consider the following questions.**

a) How do you think psychologists know that newborn babies are *well prepared to learn about their new environment?*

b) What kind of experiments do you think psychologists might have done to find out?

11.2 **Read Paragraph B of Text 2-2 to answer the following question.**

> In what ways have psychologists investigated how well prepared newborn babies are to learn from their environment?

a) Highlight the key words that give you this information.

b) Compare your key words with those of the rest of the class, and discuss why you have chosen them.

11.3 **Write a one-sentence summary using your key words, without referring back to the text. Then compare your summary with the rest of the class.**

_____

_____

_____

Task 12: Summarizing information from the text (2)

12.1 **Think about how young babies develop vision. Which of the following do you think are most visually attractive to babies?**

a) the centre or edges of objects

b) patterned or plain objects

c) curves or straight lines

d) faces or machines

12.2 **Read Paragraphs C–E to check your answers to Ex 12.1. Highlight the key words that give you this information.**

12.3 **Write a one-sentence summary of the answer to the question in Ex 12.1 using your key words, without referring back to the text. Compare your answer with a partner.**

_____

_____

_____

Text 2-3 | Hearing, taste and smell (Source Book p. 15)

This section expands on the capacities of newborn babies. There is a focus on search reading and summarizing text-based discussion.

Task 13: Using background knowledge

What can newborn babies do in terms of hearing, taste and smell? Put a tick (✔) against the following things that you think newborn babies (aged one month or less) can do.

a) ☐ Hear loud noises.

b) ☐ Turn their heads towards where a sound is coming from.

c) ☐ Correctly identify where a sound is coming from in the dark.

d) ☐ See the difference between a picture of a cat and a picture of a dog.

e) ☐ Hear the difference between two sounds that are almost the same.

f) ☐ Hear the difference between speech and non-human sounds.

g) ☐ Hear the difference between some sounds better than adults can.

h) ☐ Tell the difference between hot and cold food.

i) ☐ Taste the difference between sweet, sour and bitter-tasting things.

j) ☐ Smell the difference between their mother's milk and milk from a bottle.

k) ☐ Tell the difference between the smell of a banana and the smell of a peach.

l) ☐ Tell the difference between a nice smell and an unpleasant smell.

> **Study tip**
>
> We all use our background knowledge when reading, but a good reader will make better use of this important resource. You often know more than you think about a topic, so always try to relate what you read to what you know – or think you know. (See *Study tip* on page 29 on inferring meaning.)

Task 14: Reading for a purpose and creating a summary

14.1 **Read Text 2-3. According to the writer, which of the activities listed in Task 13 can newborn babies do? Note down anything that surprises or interests you.**

_____

_____

_____

14.2 **Discuss in groups the things you have noted in Ex 14.1 above. Refer to the text in order to support your point of view.**

14.3 **Text 2-3 suggests that babies have four innate abilities related to hearing, taste and smell. Write a short paragraph summarizing these abilities. The summary should paraphrase the explanation in the text.**

_____

_____

_____

Unit summary

In this unit you have learnt how to use the knowledge you already have of a topic before you read more about it, and to quickly identify the main points of the text that you are reading. You have also learnt to recognize key words and why they are important for helping you to achieve your reading purpose, and practised summarizing useful information that you have found in a text.

1   **Tick the statement in each pair of statements that is true for you.**

a) ☐ It is easier to read a text if I already know something about the topic.

☐ It makes no difference whether I know about the topic or not.

b) ☐ It is usually confusing to read a text if I have previously read a text on the same topic.

☐ It is easier to read a text if I have previously read something about the same topic.

c) ☐ I appreciate why it is a good idea to read for general understanding before developing further understanding.

☐ I don't understand why I shouldn't look for the specific information I need straightaway.

d) ☐ Before reading a text, I find it helpful to learn key words and phrases related to the topic.

☐ I like to think about what words and phrases mean as I read the text.

e) ☐ I know that I will need to understand key words and phrases to use them to write a summary.

☐ I can write a good summary without worrying about key words and phrases.

f) ☐ I often understand all the words and phrases but don't really understand the main argument.

☐ I can usually understand the main argument without understanding every word and phrase.

2   **Look at the topics and the list of words and phrases that relate to them. Can you recognize the one word or phrase in each list that is likely to be key to the topic?**

a) heart disease   skeleton / cardiac arrest / hospital ward / optician / painful

b) English grammar   chapter / equations / data / verb tenses / literature

c) sports injuries   fracture / score a goal / disqualification / disappointing / transfer window

d) public transport   powerful / check-in luggage / bus lanes / parking meter / overtake

e) recycling   electrical / luxury products / lead-free / waste disposal / ozone layer

---

For web resources relevant to this unit, see:

www.englishforacademicstudy.com/student/reading/links

This weblink will provide you with additional practice in developing pre-reading strategies and skills such as using existing knowledge about a topic.

3a The environment today

This unit will help you:
- read quickly for global comprehension of the main ideas in a text;
- make use of your prior knowledge to help your global comprehension;
- identify key words to enhance quick global comprehension;
- think about what strategies to use for a specific reading purpose.

In this unit you will read two texts. The first is from an article in *Geographical Review* about acid rain, and the second is from the *Biological Science Review* about the decline of one particular bird species.

Text 3a-1 | Acid rain in Norway (Source Book pp. 16–18)

Task 1: Raising text awareness

Often it is useful to be able to summarize a text quickly and efficiently without carefully reading all or nearly all of the words in the text. When you want to do a global summary of a text, you need to focus immediately on the topic. The title should help. After reading the title, you may find that you automatically draw on your prior knowledge to bring what you know about the topic to mind.

1.1 What is a global summary? Write a short definition.

_____

_____

_____

_____

1.2 Look at Text 3a-1 in the Source Book. What is the title? You have one minute to write down anything you know about acid rain.

_____

_____

_____

_____

1.3 You may also want to ask yourself questions about the title, e.g., *Is acid rain only important in Norway?* What other questions could you ask yourself about the title? Discuss your ideas with a partner.

Task 2: Taking information from displayed information

Text 3a-1 contains quite a lot of *overt* or *displayed* information, e.g., apart from the title, there are also three figures, a table and two section subheadings. Figure 1, for example, tells you that the use of lime to reduce acidification damage in Norway seems to have increased significantly between 1983 and 1995 (particularly after 1993). Therefore, certain key words may be useful here and in the other sources of *overt* information provided with this text. Terms such as *lime* and *acidification damage* are obviously important, and are phrases on which you might focus in order to gain a quick global understanding of the text.

2.1 Look through Text 3a-1. What new information (or words) do you learn from Figures 2 and 3, Table 1 and the two section subheadings? For example, what trends do the figures suggest?

Information source	New information or words
Figure 1	Very sharp rise in amount of lime used to reduce acidification damage, especially since 1993.
Figure 2	Sulphur dioxide emissions falling gradually 1975 - 1995
Figure 3	Rising nitrogen oxide emissions peaked late 1980s
Table 1	Excess deposits of sulphur halved between 1985 - 2010
Section subheading A	Rivers + lakes are damaged by acid rain
Section subheading B	Damage can be reduced

2.2 You have learnt about how to quickly access information to help you form a global summary. Discuss what you have learnt in small groups and complete the following list of points.

Ways of quickly accessing information about a text include:

- looking at the title
- section headings
- figures / tables
- 1st + last paras
- topic sentence (eg 1st sentence of a paragraph)
- pictures / captions
-

Task 3: Writing a global summary

When writing a global summary, concentrate on the main points. Write as accurately as you can, but your main aim is to communicate clearly what you understand to be the key points of a text.

3.1 **Read Text 3a-1. (Your teacher will set you a time limit for this.)**

3.2 **Write a single-paragraph summary of Text 3a-1. (Your teacher will also set a time limit for this task.)**

_____

_____

_____

_____

_____

3.3 **Compare your summary with the model supplied by your teacher.**

3.4 **Think about the strategies you used to carry out the task. Bearing in mind your teacher's summary, do you think your strategies were successful?**

a) Do you agree with your teacher's summary?

b) What strategies did you use to carry out the task?

c) Were the strategies successful?

3.5 **How do you rate your summary?**

a) Tick the score that you think best describes it: 100% ☐ 75% ☐ 50% ☐ 25% ☐

b) If you had any problems doing the task, what were they? Choose from the list below.

- Difficulty with the topic
- Difficulty with the vocabulary and/or the language
- The way the text was organized
- Difficulty with the content of the text (e.g., ideas, hypothesis, concepts, etc.)
- The length of the text
- Other reasons (not listed above)

_____

_____

Text 3a-2 Skylarks in decline (Source Book pp. 19–21)

You now have a second text to summarize. This will give you an opportunity to put into practice what you have learnt from this summary.

Task 4: More global summary practice

4.1 Read Text 3a-2, in the time limit your teacher gives you. You will not have time to read the whole text.

4.2 Write a one-paragraph summary, using your own words.

_____

_____

_____

_____

_____

_____

_____

_____

4.3 Compare your summary with the model supplied by your teacher.

4.4 Discuss the following questions.

a) In what ways was Text 3a-2 similar to or different from Text 3a-1?

b) What strategies did you employ to complete this task?

c) Were you more successful or less successful in completing the second summary?

Unit summary

In this unit you have practised reading quickly for global comprehension of the main ideas in a text in order to write a summary. You have also thought more about how you can use prior knowledge to help your global comprehension and how identifying key words can enhance this.

1 **Complete this summary about accessing information in a text by using one word only in each space.**

> If you want to access information in a text quickly and efficiently, you need to be able to quickly identify the _____ of the text – what the text is about. You won't need to understand the meaning of every _____ or phrase to do this. To start with, looking at the _____ of the text will help you to draw on your _____ knowledge and to start thinking about what the text might tell you. You might like to ask some _____ that you want the text to answer. Looking at displayed _____, like figures, tables and subheadings will help you to make further predictions and build up a picture of the text before you read. As you read, you need to be able to identify _____ points that will help you summarize the main idea or argument in the text.

2 **In this unit, you had to identify the difficulties you had when writing a successful summary. Without looking back, complete this statement.**

My biggest difficulty writing a successful summary was _____

_____ .

3 **Give one piece of advice to a classmate who wants to write a successful summary of a text.**

> For web resources relevant to this unit, see:
> **www.englishforacademicstudy.com/student/reading/links**
> This weblink will provide you with help on paraphrasing and summarizing.

Statistics without tears

This unit will help you:
- practise reading to acquire knowledge;
- learn how to distinguish between main and minor points in a text;
- summarize information from short sections of a text.

The topic of this unit is statistics. Many degree courses involve some knowledge of statistics, either because these are often quoted in academic texts, or because students have to work with statistics for their academic assignments. Furthermore, governments and other organizations often use statistics as a basis for decisions that can affect all our lives. From this point of view, some understanding of what it means to think statistically should be useful for everyone.

Text 4-1 Making sense of experience (Source Book pp. 25–28)

Task 1: Statistics in practice

1.1 **Discuss the following questions in groups. Do you agree on the answers?**

a) Kate works in an office. On Monday, she arrived at work at nine o'clock. On Tuesday, she arrived at work at nine o'clock. On Wednesday, she arrived at work at nine o'clock. On Thursday, she arrived at work at nine o'clock. What time do you think she arrived on Friday? Why?

b) Your friend wants to show you a magic trick. He tosses a coin three times, and each time it falls to the ground with heads facing up. As he goes to toss the coin again, he asks you, *Do you think it will be heads again?* And you say *No*, but when he tosses the coin, it is heads. He tosses the coin twice more, and each time it is heads again. You pick up the coin and look at both sides carefully. What do you expect to see? Why?

1.2 **Are you sure you have given the correct answers in Ex 1.1, or could you be wrong? Is it possible to be absolutely sure about such predictions? Why, or why not?**

Task 2: Identifying main and supporting points

In Task 1, you used your everyday knowledge of the world to make judgements about what things are likely or unlikely to be true, in order to make a prediction about the current situation. This is an example of everyday statistical thinking. The text you are about to read looks at what it means to think statistically in order to make predictions. Don't worry if you find statistics difficult as the text is from a book called *Statistics without tears*!

2.1 **Read Text 4-1, Section 1 in the Source Book. Which of the following are main points (write *main*) and which are minor points or examples (write *minor*)?**

a) We are naturally observant of the things around us. _____

b) Our observations often involve counting or measuring things. _____

c) Our observations may concern how big something is. _____

d) Sometimes our observations concern a single thing. _____

e) Sometimes our observations concern several things. _____

f) Observations may be made about a crop in a field. _____

g) We tend to look for connections among the things we have observed. _____

2.2 **Discuss your answers to Ex 2.1 with the rest of the class.**

2.3 **Look at the writer's question at the end of Section 1 (lines 29–30). Without reading further, write down what you think the answer is in one or two sentences. Compare your ideas with the rest of the class.**

_____

_____

_____

_____

_____

> **Study tip**
>
> It is sometimes useful to pause and think about what you have read so far. You will then be better prepared to understand information in the rest of the text.

Task 3: Continuing to identify main and minor points

3.1 **Read the first paragraph of Text 4-1, Section 2. How has the writer answered the question that was asked at the end of the previous section?**

It is important to fully understand the writer's answer, as this is a key part of what s/he wants you to learn from the text.

3.2 **Read the rest of Section 2. Which of the following are main points (write *main*) and which are minor points or examples (write *minor*)? Discuss your answers with the rest of the class.**

a) Statistics aim to help us make sense of our observations. _____

b) Statistics aim to help us avoid jumping to conclusions. _____

c) Statistics aim to help us be cautious about making generalizations. _____

d) A field was treated with a certain fertilizer and produced a big crop. _____

e) Perhaps other fields treated with the same fertilizer will produce big crops. _____

3.3 **Look at the writer's question at the end of Section 2 (lines 48–49). Without reading further, write down what you think the answer is in one or two sentences.**

_____

_____

_____

_____

_____

Task 4: Summarizing the key points (1)

4.1 Read the first paragraph of Text 4-1, Section 3. How has the writer answered the question that was asked at the end of the previous section?

As with the answer to the previous question, this is an important part of what the author wants you to learn.

4.2 Read the rest of Section 3. Complete the following summaries of the main ideas in the text. Use a word or phrase from the box and write the correct number in each gap in the sentences that follow.

1	a certain kind of field
2	a mistake
3	correct
4	different kinds of field
5	difficult calculations
6	likelihood (or 'probability')
7	more confident
8	no 100% certainties
9	experience
10	more scientific

Study tip

Like all reading skills, summarizing will develop with practice. Make sure you continue to make use of this skill after working through these practice activities. For example, you can use the 'recall' method to quickly write down or even tell someone what you have just read. This will help you make sense of your reading, and evaluate how much you have understood.

a) It could be __2__ to conclude that because one field produced a large crop, other fields treated in the same way will do the same.

b) The more observations we make, the _____ we can be about our generalizations.

c) _____ is a very important concept in statistics.

d) Likelihood (or 'probability') refers to the idea that there are _____ in statistics.

e) _____ treated in a certain way may generally produce a bigger potato crop, but this may not always happen.

4.3 Discuss your answers to Ex 4.2 with another student.

4.4 Look at the writer's question at the end of Section 3 (lines 72–77). Without reading further, write down what you think the answer is in one or two sentences.

_____

_____

_____

_____

40   English for academic study

Task 5: Summarizing the key points (2)

5.1 Read the first paragraph of Text 4-1, Section 4. How has the writer answered the question that was asked at the end of the previous section?

5.2 Read the rest of Section 4. Complete the gaps in the following summary of the main points, using words from Section 4.

Statistics involves finding _____ patterns among things we observe.
However, we should not assume that _____ will all follow these patterns.
The two main concerns of statistics are:
- summarizing our _____;
- making _____ based on the reading summary.

Text 4-2 What is statistics? (Source Book pp. 29–30)

You are going to read a second extract from the book. This has just one section.

Task 6: Concentrating on the main points

6.1 Read Text 4-2, Section 5, and make a list of the main points on a separate sheet of paper. You may find it easier to make three lists, following the divisions shown below.

Lines 90–109
Statistics is used in four different senses.
_____
_____

Lines 110–122
Most professional activities use statistical thinking.
_____
_____

Lines 123–140
Statistics is used because of uncertainty about our observations.
_____
_____

Text 4-3 Descriptive and inferential statistics (Source Book pp. 31–33)

You are going to read a third extract from the book. This has just two subsections.

Task 7: Note-taking practice

7.1 Read Text 4-3, Section 6. Look at the writer's question at the end of the section. Write down what you think the answer is, in one or two sentences.

_____

_____

_____

_____

_____

7.2 Compare your ideas with the rest of the class.

7.3 Read the first paragraph of Text 4-3, Section 7. How has the writer answered the question asked at the end of the previous section?

7.4 Read the rest of Section 7. Makes notes or annotate parts of the text to prepare for writing a summary.

You are reading Section 7 to find out what the writer says about the distinctions between descriptive and inferential statistics, and the reliability of making generalizations.

7.5 Write a short summary, using your notes from Ex 7.4.

_____

_____

_____

_____

_____

_____

_____

_____

Task 8: Recalling information from the text

Recalling information that you have previously read is a useful strategy for improving your understanding of a text.

8.1 **Put away Text 4-3 and any notes you have made. With a partner, try to recall from memory the main points in Section 7, using the words in the box to help you.**

descriptive statistics   inferential statistics   population generalization   sample observation   representative   reliability

8.2 **Check through the text to see if you have forgotten any important information.**

8.3 **Write a short summary of Section 7, using the following two headings.**

- Distinctions between descriptive and inferential statistics
- The reliability of making generalizations

_____

_____

_____

_____

_____

_____

_____

_____

_____

_____

_____

_____

8.4 **Discuss and compare your summaries in small groups.**

8.5 **Compare your summary with the one given to you by your teacher. Have you selected similar main points?**

Unit summary

In this unit you have practised reading to acquire knowledge and learnt how to distinguish between main and minor points in a text. You have also practised summarizing information from short sections of a text.

1 **Divide the following words into two categories. Write them into the correct half of the box below.**

minor   main   key   supporting   important

2 **Look at these two topics and the list of points. Can you identify the ONE main point and the two supporting points in each? Tick the main point.**

Growing populations in the world's biggest cities

a) ☐ Quickly built shanty towns have no electricity or hot water.

b) ☐ There are hundreds of thousands of new arrivals each month.

c) ☐ It is almost impossible to control crime in some of the poorest areas.

Sports injuries

a) ☐ Sports injuries can be broadly classified as either traumatic or overuse injuries.

b) ☐ A bruise is damage to small blood vessels which causes bleeding.

c) ☐ The inflammatory stage typically lasts about five days.

3 **Delete the wrong option in each statement below so that it is true for you.**

a) I find it *easy / quite easy / quite difficult / very difficult* to quickly identify the main points in a text.

b) I find it *easy / quite easy / quite difficult / very difficult* to distinguish between main points and minor points.

c) I find it *easy / quite easy / quite difficult / very difficult* to concentrate on the main points as I read.

d) I find it *easy / quite easy / quite difficult / very difficult* to summarize the main points of a text.

e) I find it *easy / quite easy / quite difficult / very difficult* to later recall the main points of a text I have read.

For web resources relevant to this unit, see:

www.englishforacademicstudy.com/student/reading/links

These weblinks will provide you with additional practice in identifying the main idea in a text and dealing with graphs and charts.

5 Human activity and climate change

This unit will help you:
- learn how to overview a text before reading, to assess its value;
- read selectively to identify words that might provide relevant information;
- practise *writing into reading* as a technique for increasing understanding of a text;
- identify topic sentences in a paragraph and recognize the supporting sentences;
- learn text-mapping as a means of enhancing understanding;
- make use of graphs, figures and tables to increase understanding of content.

In this unit you will read three texts about climate change and whether man's activities have had a significant impact. The texts come from a brochure co-sponsored by the United Nations Environmental Programme (UNEP) and the World Meteorological Organization (WMO).

Text 5-1 | Extra-textual information (Source Book p. 34)

Focus task

Your main reason for reading Texts 5-1, 5-2 and 5-3 is to prepare a set of notes using relevant information from the texts in order either to write an essay or to give a presentation about the following topic.

> What role has human activity played in causing climate change?

Before reading the text itself, you are going to look at some additional information included in the brochure, e.g., names of contributing authors and who they work for.

Task 1: Overviewing the text

The purpose of overviewing the text is to help make quick decisions about the particular value of the text to the reader. Overviewing saves time. Two ways of doing this are:

- to briefly look at any other extra-textual information (e.g., the blurb);
- to pay attention to the content of the Introduction.

1.1 Can you think of other ways of overviewing the text? List them below.

_____

_____

_____

_____

_____

1.2 Below is a list of questions which might be asked about a text before reading it. Find the answers by overviewing the whole document.

  a) What is the text about?

  b) Who is/are the author(s) of the text? What is their background?

  c) Why was the text written?

  d) What type of text is it?

  e) Will the text be useful or relevant for carrying out the Focus task?

Text 5-2 | Common questions about climate change (Source Book pp. 35–36)

This section of the text provides general information on the topic of climate change, including the role of human activity.

Task 2: Writing into reading

One effective way of fully understanding a text is to *write your way into reading*. This works by activating knowledge you may already have about the topic to help you improve your understanding of the text when you actually read it. *Writing into reading* involves writing down your own ideas about the topic, e.g., as a quick list, before attempting to read it.

2.1 Make a list of human activities that you think might have contributed to climate change. Tick (✔) any activities that you have had personal experience of.

_____

_____

_____

_____

2.2 Compare your list with a partner and agree on a master list, i.e., the items on which you both agree.

2.3 Scan Text 5-2 and compare information in the text with your list.

Look for appropriate information about the impact of human activities on climate change.

Task 3: Identifying topic sentences

Paragraphs often contain a sentence which summarizes the main point of each particular paragraph. These are called *topic sentences* and you can usually identify them through position and content. Topic sentences help the reader quickly grasp the main ideas in a text.

Discuss the following with a partner.

a) Where would you expect the topic sentence to appear:

- the first sentence?
- the final sentence?
- in the middle of the paragraph?

b) What is the function of the other sentences that appear in each paragraph?

> **Study tip**
>
> When reading for the gist of a text; it is very helpful to identify the topic sentences in each paragraph as these provide a summary of the rest of the content.

Task 4: Understanding the general meaning of a text

4.1 Look at Paragraph A of Text 5-2. Pay attention to the sentence in lines 5–6. What are the issues? Number these issues (1–3).

4.2 Scan through the text and number the paragraphs 1, 2 or 3, depending on which issue they deal with.

4.3 Which paragraph(s) look(s) ahead to the future?

4.4 What is the purpose of the final paragraph?

Task 5: Topic sentences and supporting sentences

In this task, you will practise *careful reading* in order to differentiate the topic sentence from supporting sentences in each paragraph. *Careful reading* involves reading most of the words in the text in order to fully understand what is written.

> **Study tip**
>
> Careful reading is one of the seven important reading strategies detailed in the introduction. It is particularly useful when differentiating between main ideas in the text and supporting ideas or details.

5.1 Read Paragraph A. The underlined sentence is the topic sentence of the paragraph.

a) Why is this the topic sentence of the Introduction?

b) What is the purpose of the first sentence?

5.2 Underline the topic sentences in each of the remaining paragraphs (B–I). With a partner, discuss the role of the other sentences in each paragraph.

5.3 According to your understanding of the text, which of the following are main ideas (write A) and which are supporting ideas or details (write B)?

a) ☐ Rapid daily weather changes can occur even in areas of unchanging climate.

b) ☐ The Earth's surface temperature would be significantly cooler without a natural greenhouse effect.

c) ☐ The effects of the wind and the oceans determine the redistribution of heat over the Earth's surface.

d) ☐ Volcanic eruptions have a temporary cooling effect.

e) ☐ One of the causes of climate change is human activity.

f) ☐ The effects of natural greenhouse gases, combined with human activity, lead to higher average Earth temperatures.

g) ☐ The rise in the average global temperature will persist for a long period as a result of man's activities.

h) ☐ The Second Assessment Report released by the IPCC is very long and detailed.

INTERGOVERNMENTAL PANEL ON CLIMATE CHANGE

IPCC Second Assessment
Climate Change 1995

A REPORT OF THE
INTERGOVERNMENTAL PANEL ON CLIMATE CHANGE

Study tip

When you are reading, it is essential to differentiate between the main ideas in the text and the supporting ideas or details.

Task 6: Recalling the text

This task involves recalling the contents of the text from memory. The idea behind this reading strategy is that after reading the text, you write down what you have understood from it. As a result, you may discover that you have understood more than you originally believed. Secondly, you will more easily recognize gaps in your understanding and recognize which parts of the text to concentrate on when rereading.

Study tip

Recalling a text from memory is a very useful reading strategy to help you monitor and improve your ability to understand the text.

6.1 **Without looking back at the text, list the main points.**
Your teacher will only give you a few minutes to complete this task, so write quickly in note form.

_____

_____

_____

_____

_____

_____

6.2 Compare your list with a partner and agree a master list, i.e., the items on which you both agree.

6.3 Check with the text. Revise your list if necessary.

6.4 Which of the points on your list are relevant to completing the Focus task on page 45? Place a tick (✔) beside all the relevant points you have listed above.

Text 5-3 Are human activities contributing to climate change? (Source Book pp. 37–39)

This section appears to contain what you need to answer the Focus task, but you will need to confirm this.

Task 7: Identifying relevant information in a text

7.1 Read Text 5-3 in the Source Book to confirm whether it will help in the completion of the Focus task on page 45.

7.2 Reread Paragraph A. What do you consider to be the key point made by the author?

_____

_____

_____

7.3 What word(s) in Paragraph A suggest(s) that this claim should be taken seriously?

_____

7.4 Search through Paragraphs B–M and highlight areas of the text which might be of use in completing the Focus task.
Use a pencil to tick (✔) or bracket appropriate sections.

Study tip

When highlighting a text, use a pencil rather than a highlighter because you may find you change your mind about the information at a later stage.

7.5 Which paragraph(s) in Text 5-3 give(s) a clear indication of the contribution of human activity to climate change?
Note that there is, in fact, limited information about the importance of human activity in this text.

_____

_____

_____

7.6 Now identify any paragraph in which the contribution of human activity to climate change is less clearly stated.
You will need to use inference to identify this information.

Study tip

A lot of information contained in a text is implied rather than clearly stated. You will need to learn how to interpret such information.

_____

_____

_____

_____

_____

7.7 In Paragraph B, what suggests the difficulty that scientists have in analyzing the problem?

_____

_____

7.8 In Paragraph E, what information might make the reader concerned about the way the data was collected?

_____

_____

7.9 In Paragraph K, what connection can be made between the comparison of _observed patterns of temperature change_ and those _predicted by models_ and the role of human activity on global change?

_____

_____

_____

_____

_____

_____

_____

_____

Task 8: Detailed reading

A significant amount of Text 5-3 is not directly relevant to the Focus task, despite this being the main purpose for reading the document. However, it may be useful to study other parts of the text quite carefully to help your understanding of the topic.

8.1   An important function of Text 5-3 is to answer the question: *Are human activities contributing to climate change?* **What other function(s) does the text have?**

_____

_____

_____

_____

_____

_____

8.2   **Complete the following summary by filling the gaps with either one or two words. The words you need are all used in the original text.**

Studying climate change

Studying the causes of unusual climate change is problematic because change caused

by _____ is often hidden or masked by natural climate

variability. In order to separate these two factors, investigations can be divided into

_____ and _____ studies. In the first case, information

can be gained by measuring _____, and in the second

situation by finding reasons for the unusual changes in climate that have been noted.

In attributing causes resulting from human activity, scientists can make use of

_____. Two examples of this are, firstly, by comparing maps or

patterns of temperature change, which is known as _____,

or secondly, by finding characteristic patterns of climate response between observed

climate change and predicted change from models, which is referred to as a

_____.

Task 9: Recalling the text from memory

9.1 Without looking back at Text 5-3, list all the key points (based on the main ideas). Write your list as quickly as possible, noting down the ideas as you think of them. You can rearrange these later if you wish.

Example: Climate change caused by human activity, e.g., burning fossil fuels

_____

_____

_____

_____

_____

_____

9.2 Compare your list with another student and agree on a master list. Place a tick (✔) beside the key points you agree on. Refer to the text to consider any further key information that you have omitted.

Text 5-4 | What human activities contribute to climate change? (Source Book pp. 40–41)

Apart from the text, this section contains two figures (Fig 3.1 and 3.2). You can understand a great deal by carefully studying graphs, diagrams, illustrations and tables. Such figures are intended to summarize the content of what you are reading.

Task 10: Making use of figures and tables

10.1 Study Figure 3.1 in Text 5-4. With a partner, discuss what conclusions can be made from this diagram. For example:

a) Compare the relative importance of climate change caused by carbon dioxide and by methane.

b) Discuss what contributions the greenhouse gases described in Figure 3.1 have made to climate change.

> **Study tip**
>
> By paying attention to the visual aids such as graphs, diagrams and illustrations, you will get a much clearer understanding of the text.

10.2 To what extent does the displayed data in Figure 3.1 help you to answer this question?

> What human activities contribute to climate change?

10.3 Read through Text 5-4 and locate the sections that refer to each of the gases displayed in Figure 3.1. Underline the names of the gases as you locate them.

Task 11: Reading displayed information

Study Figure 3.2. What conclusions can be made about the contents of this figure? Answer the following questions to help you make appropriate conclusions.

a) What is the general trend for all three groups of countries?

_____

_____

_____

b) Which group of countries was contributing the most to climate change by 1992?

_____

_____

_____

c) What future trends are suggested by the graph? Read through Text 5-4 to find which paragraph(s) are related to Figure 3.2.

_____

_____

_____

Task 12: Inferring meaning from a text

12.1 **Reread Text 5-4 and find references to the following phrases. What is their significance regarding climate change?**

Example: The burning of fossil fuels = *very significant contributor to carbon dioxide emissions*

a) The regrowth of vegetation in the Northern hemisphere

b) Land use changes

c) Existing international agreements

d) The tropospheric zone

e) The Antarctic ozone hole

f) Small particles in the atmosphere

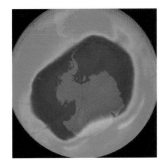

12.2 What general conclusions can be made about Text 5-4? Write your conclusions below.

_____

_____

_____

_____

_____

_____

_____

_____

_____

_____

_____

_____

Task 13: Making use of a text

You should now be ready to return to the Focus task on the first page of this unit (page 45). Reread this task and decide what information you can use from the three texts in order to prepare notes for an oral presentation, or a plan for a writing assignment.

13.1 Prepare and organize your notes as directed by your teacher.

13.2 Explain the contents and organization of your notes to a partner.

13.3 Give an oral presentation or complete a writing assignment, as your teacher advises.

Unit summary

In this unit you have learnt how to overview a text to assess its particular value. You have practised reading for a specific purpose and reading selectively to identify words which might provide information relevant to a specific purpose. You have also practised strategies to improve reading comprehension, which include writing into reading, identifying topic sentences and supporting sentences, text-mapping and making use of displayed information.

1 **Cover Ex 2 and answer these questions as quickly as you can.**

   a) What do you do if you *overview a text*?

   b) What does *writing your way into reading* mean?

   c) What is a *topic sentence*?

   d) What are *supporting sentences*?

   e) What is *text-mapping*?

2 **Match the sentence beginnings a–h with the sentence endings 1–8.**

   a) ☐ If I overview a text, it will …

   b) ☐ If I ask questions about a text before I read, it will …

   c) ☐ If I practice *writing into reading*, it will …

   d) ☐ If I look carefully at displayed information like graphs and tables, it will …

   e) ☐ If I can quickly identify topic sentences, it will …

   f) ☐ If I can differentiate between topic sentences and supporting sentences, it will …

   g) ☐ If I write down key points from a text after I have read it, it might …

   h) ☐ If I use a pencil to highlight points in a text, it will …

   1 make me realize that I understand more than I thought and help me to identify what I didn't understand.

   2 help me to summarize in a way that I might not be able to do by reading the text alone.

   3 help me to activate prior knowledge and to understand more of the content.

   4 help me decide what I want to find out from reading it.

   5 save time and help me to make quick decisions about its particular value.

   6 be easier to go back and make changes if I need to.

   7 help me read more carefully and to understand the organization of a paragraph better.

   8 help me know what information is key and what is detail.

For web resources relevant to this unit, see:

www.englishforacademicstudy.com/student/reading/links

These weblinks will provide you with further practice in note-taking as well as information on the topic of climate change.

The global village

This unit will help you:
- practise recognizing main points in a text;
- read for a specific purpose;
- analyze the titles, subtitles (subheadings) and other displayed accompanying information;
- recall the text to consolidate your understanding;
- compare your views (as a reader) with those of the writer;
- monitor your understanding of the text while you are reading.

In this unit you will read up to six sections of a text called *The global village* about the effects of globalization on the world we live in.

Text 6-1 | Introduction (Source Book pp. 42–43)

This introduction will give you an overview of the text.

Task 1: Pre-reading discussion

1.1 **The term *global village* was first used by the Canadian academic Marshall McLuhan.**

   a) Discuss in groups what this term might mean.

   b) Compare your group's definition with your teacher's definition. How similar are they?

1.2 **Consider some of the characteristics of the *global village* from your teacher's definition. Make a list of the ways that you think they may have affected your life.**

   Example:

> You are studying abroad and you may consider this to be a direct (or indirect) result of globalization.

1.3 **Compare your list with other members of your group.**

Task 2: Checking predictions

2.1 **Read Text 6-1 in the Source Book. Are any of the points mentioned by the author similar to the points you listed in Ex 1.2?**

   As you read:
   - underline with a <u>solid line</u> any ideas in the text that are similar to the ones that you have on your list;
   - underline with a <u>broken line</u> any ideas in the text which are not on your list.

2.2 **Compare your list with a partner.**

Text 6-2 The shrinking planet (Source Book pp. 44–45)

This is the first of five sections and it will provide you with information on one aspect of the global village.

Task 3: Thinking about the topic

3.1 **The title of Text 6-2 is *The shrinking planet*. What do you think this means?**
Remember that the overall theme of the text is *The global village*.

3.2 **In what ways do you think trade, tourism and technology lessen the differences between people in different parts of the world?**

Global brand names, e.g., Coca-Cola

3.3 **Think about the effects of globalization on the differences between cultures around the world.**

a) Do you think that some differences between people in different parts of the world may be maintained in spite of globalization, or even increased because of it?

b) If so, what examples can you think of?

3.4 Look at the words and expressions from Text 6-2 in the box below. Check you understand what they mean, using a dictionary if necessary.

> ~~discontent~~   cultural convergence   the Internet   grievances
> alien modern cultures   universal links   superficial   national culture, history and language
> common interests   similar products   human peculiarities   homogenizing effect
> customization of products   local requirements   digital technology

3.5 Place the words and expressions in the appropriate column in the table below.

For example, *discontent* would probably cause *divergence*.

Convergence	Divergence
	discontent

3.6 In groups, discuss what you think the text will be about.

Task 4: Recalling the text from memory

4.1 Read the subheading of Text 6-2 and answer the following questions.

a) What is the function of this subheading and what does it mean?

_____

_____

_____

_____

_____

b)   What contrast is suggested by this subheading?

_____

_____

_____

_____

_____

4.2   Read Text 6-2. Why does the writer feel that *many cultural differences persist*?

4.3   Work in pairs and recall the text from memory by telling each other what you remember. Some of the words and expressions in Ex 3.4 may help you.

Study tip

Recalling the text helps you to consolidate your understanding of a text. It also helps you to appreciate what you have not understood.

4.4   Reread Text 6-2 to check your answers to Ex 4.3. Did you forget any important points? Were there any inaccuracies?

Task 5: Checking the text for details

This task will help you have a more detailed understanding of the text.

Read Text 6-2 again, then annotate the statements below as follows.

● If the statement is correct according to the text, write *Yes*.

● If the statement is not correct, write *No*.

● If you cannot find any information relating to the statement, write *Not given*.

a) _____ A surprising number of people in the world are able to watch TV.

b) _____ In 1998, Ronaldo, a young Brazilian footballer, was much better known internationally than President Clinton.

c) _____ Increasing numbers of Africans are migrating to the United States.

d) _____ Some people use the Internet as a method for making political protests.

e) _____ Books about Canada are frequently written in Spanish.

f) _____ There is a football team in Tanzania which has adopted the name Manchester United.

g) _____ An increasing number of young people in China have little or no knowledge of their national heritage.

h) _____ As a result of computer technology, more and more people throughout the world are driving exactly the same basic model of car.

i) _____ Digital technology seems to be reversing the effect of globalization.

j) _____ The writer is negative about the effects of globalization.

Task 6: Making use of the text content

6.1 **Discuss the following question in groups, and note the results of your discussion in the table below.**

The data you gather may be useful in carrying out the summarizing activity that is introduced in the next task (on page 61).

> Assuming that you are part of the global village, what cultural differences persist in your class (if any)?

Attitude about:	The same attitude?	Different attitude?
Study methods		
Studying abroad		
Entertainment		
Foreign goods		
International languages		
National culture		

6.2 **What conclusions can be drawn from the information you collected in Ex 6.1?**

Focus task

The aim of this Focus task is to provide an overall purpose for using *all* the texts in this unit. It will provide practice in making decisions about what to read and how carefully to read it. It will also provide an opportunity to practise your note-taking techniques. The topic is:

> Has social diversity generally increased as the result of economic globalization?

Based on your own experience and the experience of other members of your group, to what extent do you agree that social diversity has generally increased? What evidence exists in the texts to support your answer?

Task 7: Reading for a purpose

7.1 Think about the Focus task and decide on the most appropriate way to carry out this task. Discuss your ideas in small groups.

7.2 Look through Texts 6-1 to 6-6 (including any texts not yet referred to) and decide which parts of each text you could use to complete this assignment.
Remember to look for relevant information.

7.3 Underline ideas in each text that appear to *support* the statement with a <u>solid line</u>. Underline ideas that *do not support* the statement with a <u>broken line</u>.

7.4 Think about what should be included in the summary. What ideas have the title of the assignment and your reading of all the texts given you? Individually, or in groups, make a list of points to include in the summary.
Remember to consider the data you collected in Ex 6.1.

_____

_____

_____

_____

Text 6-3 | Economic globalization (Source Book pp. 45–47)

Task 8: Asking questions about the text

The aim of this section is to look more closely at Text 6-3 and decide how relevant the content is with regard to completing the Focus task. This is also an opportunity to reconsider the highlighting/note-taking you did in Task 7. You may wish to change or add to your highlighting as you go through Text 6-3.

8.1 Look at the following questions. Read Text 6-3 and underline the words or phrases which answer these questions.

a) What inconsistency is expressed in the section entitled *The global marketplace*? (Use no more than ten words.)

b) What two things have increased dramatically because of economic globalization?

c) What two services, mentioned in Paragraph B, have been globalized?

d) What three international agreements and organizations have affected economic globalization?

e) What four factors have hampered economic globalization?

> **Study tip**
>
> One way of getting a better understanding of the text when reading carefully is to ask yourself questions about the text as you read.

f) What is done in some countries to protect the workforce?

g) Why does the expansion of international trade cause even some well-managed businesses to fail?

h) In what ways is the pre-industrial village different from the global village? (Use no more than ten words.)

i) Which countries benefit most from economic globalization?

j) In what three ways has economic globalization had a negative effect on richer countries? (Use no more than ten words per point.)

k) What positive long-term factors does the writer identify in the final paragraph?

8.2 **Can you think of any other questions you could ask that would help you understand the text?**

_____

_____

_____

_____

_____

8.3 **With a partner, decide how relevant your answers to Ex 8.1 are to the Focus task.**

Task 9: Identifying key information in the text

This task will help you check your understanding of the main point of each paragraph in Text 6-3.

Sentences 1–8 below summarize Paragraphs A–H of Text 6-3. Match each of these sentences with the appropriate paragraph letter from the text.

A = ☐ **B =** ☐ **C =** ☐ **D =** ☐
E = ☐ **F =** ☐ **G =** ☐ **H =** ☐

1 There are a number of factors which may delay the process of globalization.

2 The differences between people become less important as a result of economic globalization.

3 Several corporate household names exemplify current global trends.

4 International free trade is directed by global agreements and covers a far greater range of commodities than was traditional.

5 The developed world continues to dominate the process of globalization.

6 Economic power does not necessarily dictate policy when human issues stand in its way.

7 The size of foreign investment and the globalization of service industries are clearly demonstrated in most areas of the world.

8 Concentration of economic power is tending to cause greater tension between the rich and the poor.

Task 10: Preparing to complete the Focus task

10.1 Review the answers to Tasks 8 and 9.

10.2 Revise your list of points relevant to the Focus task (Ex 7.4). Add any new points you have found to your list.

10.3 In groups, compare your lists. Refer to the text where necessary to check your points.

Text 6-4 | Community & conflict (Source Book pp. 48–50)

The next text consists of a main body text (Paragraphs A–H) and three short accompanying texts that provide further comment about the topic. These are in separate boxes.

Task 11: Thinking about the topic

The text outlines some of the social effects that globalization has on individual societies. It will be helpful to discuss what you know about this subject before reading the next section.

11.1 Think about the title of Text 6-4: *Community & conflict*. What does this suggest about the contents of the text?

_____

_____

_____

11.2 Make a list of five causes of conflict in modern society on an international/global scale. **Example:**

border disputes between two countries where one or both countries accuse the

other of stealing some of their land.

_____

_____

_____

_____

11.3 What 'community' do you think the writer is referring to in the title of Text 6-4? Read the subtitle and the note *Global village – global inequality*. What implication is made regarding the possibility of conflict?

Task 12: Developing understanding of the text

12.1 Read the subtitle of Text 6-4. Who are the citizens of the global village? Read Text 6-4 and highlight any words or phrases which might indicate certain characteristics or features of the typical *citizen*.

Example: *better educated*

12.2 Make brief notes on the types of global community mentioned in Text 6-4.

Task 13: Identifying relevant information for the Focus task

You will have to decide whether the contents of Text 6-4 are relevant to the Focus task assignment (page 60). But first you have to evaluate what it has to say about conflict, the heading of this section.

13.1 Read through Text 6-4 and highlight or annotate sections of the text which relate to conflict.

13.2 Compare your annotations with the list you compiled for Ex 11.2. Decide whether the points on your list are similar to the points raised in the text. Discuss the points listed in groups.

13.3 Decide whether Text 6-4 is relevant to the Focus task (page 60). Do you think that the social diversity mentioned in Text 6-4 is a result of economic factors?

13.4 Think about the causes of conflict mentioned in the text that you have already annotated. In what ways, if any, are the points you highlighted in Ex 13.2 related to economic globalization?

13.5 In groups, list any points which you consider relevant to the Focus task. Compare your answers with another group.

Task 14: Completing an assignment

14.1 Write a two-paragraph summary of the main ideas you would use to complete the following assignment.

> Has social diversity generally increased as a result of economic globalization?
>
> To what extent do you think social diversity has increased? What evidence exists with reference to the texts selected from The global village: Challenges for a shrinking planet?

You might want to make use of the following techniques.

- Recalling the texts immediately after reading them to check your understanding.
- Asking yourself questions as you read through the texts, as you practised with Text 6-3.
- Identifying topic sentences or main ideas as you read.
- Skimming through the texts first and then reading them more carefully (or selected parts which seem more relevant) and annotating certain key ideas or words.

Text 6-5 The sharing of sovereignty (Source Book pp. 50–52)

Text 6-6 Converging or diverging? (Source Book pp. 53–55)

These are two more texts from the same source that follow Text 6-4.

14.2 Read Texts 6-5 and 6-6 in the Source Book and decide whether or not these will be useful to you in completing the Focus task.

You will find it useful when reading and thinking about these texts to employ some of the reading strategies that you have practised in this unit and in earlier units.

Unit summary

In this unit you have learnt how to apply the reading skills you have learnt so far to reading with the aim of selecting key information from a number of sources. You have also learnt how to monitor your understanding of the text while you are reading and you have compared your views (as a reader) with those of the writer.

1 **Use your notebook to write one thing that you think you have improved and one thing that you still find difficult when you are trying to apply each of the following reading strategies.**

a) making predictions about the content of a text

b) learning key vocabulary that will occur in a text before reading the text

c) reading for detailed information

d) recalling the text from memory

2 **Which of the following reading strategies did you find especially helpful when selecting information from a number of sources in order to complete the Focus task? Tick three.**

- [ ] overviewing each text before reading
- [ ] asking yourself questions about the content of each text before reading
- [ ] making predictions about the content of each text before reading
- [ ] skimming each text quickly before reading more carefully
- [ ] highlighting points in each text in different ways (solid line / broken line, for example)
- [ ] writing down a list of key points from each text
- [ ] asking yourself questions about the text as you read
- [ ] trying to recall key points from each text before reading again to check

3 **Complete the following summary with some of the words from the box.**

> If the Focus task asks you to express an opinion, you will need to select
> _____ information from the texts you read that _____
> your answer. If you choose to express an opinion based on your own _____
> or that of people you know, you will need to make sure that you provide
> _____ to back up what you say.

logic	essential	evidence	convince	relevant	experience	support

For web resources relevant to this unit, see:
www.englishforacademicstudy.com/student/reading/links

These weblinks will provide additional help in developing strategies to strengthen your comprehension skills, as well as information on the topic of globalization.

7 The new linguistic order

This unit will help you:
- read an article on 'the new linguistic order' and use it to complete an assignment;
- practise making use of a specific text to support your ideas;
- develop the skills you have learnt so far on this reading course.

In this unit you will read an article that appeared in the journal *Foreign Policy*. You will make use of the contents of the article to complete an assignment. You will therefore be approaching the text in the same way as you will be expected to on many academic courses, i.e., *reading to learn* rather than *learning to read*.

Reading assignment

> What future significant language developments might occur in a country such as Zambia?

Discuss this topic with special reference to Text 7-1: *The new linguistic order*.

Task 1: Deciding how to read a text

You will have to make certain decisions about how to approach Text 7-1. For example, you need to be selective about the information that you will use. Obviously, the information should be relevant to the Focus task. This should lead you to make decisions about the text.

- Should you read the whole text first before making any notes, or should you annotate the text as you read?
- Should you look quickly at the headings in the text and read only the parts which seem relevant to the assignment?
- Should you check every word you don't understand? If not, how should you deal with unknown vocabulary?

Individually or in groups, make a list of other decisions you need to make about how to read the text.

Task 2: Reading an introductory case study

Before reading the main article, you are going to read a short text and discuss the importance of English in Zambia and the future English will have in countries like Zambia. This short text provides some background information relevant to the current use of English in Zambia.

2.1 **Read through the introduction to the text on page 68 and note down four points about the language situation in Zambia that you consider to be particularly important.**

LANGUAGES IN ZAMBIA

Zambia is a developing landlocked country situated in Central Africa. The population, approximately 9.7 million, is made up of 98.7 per cent African people, 1.1 per cent European and 0.2 per cent other (*The World Factbook*, 1999 – Zambia). The African population consists of four main tribal groups. There are also a number of subsidiary groups. As a result, there is a wide variety of tribal languages and dialects. There is also a significant number of other permanent residents in Zambia whose first language is not a Zambian tribal language or dialect. For example, there are first-language speakers of English, Swahili, Hindi and Afrikaans. Because of this, it has been necessary for Zambia to have a common language of communication for a range of social, political, educational, technical and economic reasons. Zambia is part of Anglophone Africa, and therefore the common language (lingua franca) is English. Approximately 78 per cent of the population over the age of 15 can read and write English. There are also at least seven major dominant vernacular languages and approximately 70 other indigenous languages.

Zambia is surrounded by neighbouring countries, each having a major European lingua franca as well as official tribal languages. These countries are Tanzania, Malawi, Zimbabwe and Namibia, where the lingua franca is English; Angola and Mozambique (Portuguese) and the Democratic Republic of Congo (formerly Zaire), where the lingua franca is French. In all these countries, therefore, like Zambia, there is multilingualism, e.g., Zambians communicate through the lingua franca as well as through at least one of the official vernacular languages. Several of the local languages transcend borders. For example, Bemba is spoken in Northern Zambia and in the south of the Democratic Republic of Congo; Nyanja in Eastern Zambia and Malawi, etc.

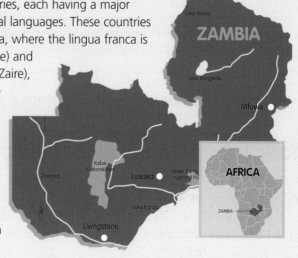

2.2 In groups, compare the points you noted in Ex 2.1. Discuss the possible significance of the following.

- The existence of other lingua francas on Zambia's borders.
- Local languages that overlap the borders of Zambia and her neighbours.
- Local languages that continue to be spoken by the vast majority of Zambians.

2.3 Look at the following possible developments and prioritize them in order from 1 to 5 (1 = *most likely*, 5 = *least likely*). In groups, discuss the order you have chosen.

IN THE FUTURE

- [ ] English will take over entirely as the only language spoken in Zambia.
- [ ] Language conflicts will develop between English speakers and other language communities.
- [ ] English will increasingly become the language of the elite, and non-fluent speakers will be seriously disadvantaged.
- [ ] The situation is likely to remain as it is, i.e., multilingualism with languages coexisting in order to serve different purposes.
- [ ] English will be replaced by some other official language.

You are now going to read Text 7-1. As you read, you will need to think about what information would be relevant for completing the following assignment:

> What future significant language developments might occur in a country such as Zambia?

You will need to make notes as you are reading and will have to make decisions about how to do this. By the end of the unit, you will be expected to have produced notes on part of the text relevant to the assignment.

Tasks 3 and 4 will make use of the first part of the text in shorter stages before the main reading focus in Task 5.

2.4 **Read Text 7-1 in the Source Book. As you read, think about what information would be relevant to the Focus task and make notes.**

Task 3: Understanding subject-specific vocabulary

It is normal in an academic situation for a student to have a working vocabulary of a particular subject or topic that has been learnt either from the lecture or seminar environment or from reading subject materials. Such a working vocabulary of subject-specific words should help the reader understand any relevant text they are asked to read.

3.1 **Read Paragraphs A–C and find the words or phrases in the box. Then match them with the definitions a–e below.**

> **1** mother tongue   **2** globalization   **3** official language
>
> **4** regionalization   **5** local language

a) ☐ A process in which a language is used in neighbouring countries, particularly for business or official reasons, but also for educational, social or recreational purposes.

b) ☐ This is used in business, in government and law courts; it may also be the national language.

c) ☐ Used in part of a country or region mostly as a first language, usually for personal, social or commercial reasons; sometimes for official or educational reasons.

d) ☐ The first language to be acquired at home.

e) ☐ A process involving worldwide interaction in trade, politics, recreation, education, etc.

3.2 **The following terms (1–10) all appear in Text 7-1. In groups, discuss what these terms mean, then try to match them with the definitions a–j.**

> **1** first language   **2** pidgin   **3** multilingual   **4** lingua franca   **5** vernacular
>
> **6** minority language   **7** working language   **8** immersion language
>
> **9** neologism   **10** standardized language

a) ☐ An internationally used language of communication, e.g., English or French in Africa.

b) ☐ Referring to a language spoken by a significant number of the population (for example, a tribal language), but not the official or national language.

c) ☐ The use of three or more languages by an individual or a group of speakers.

d) ☐ A language used 'comfortably' by speakers for specific purposes, e.g., for study, trade or diplomacy.

e) ☐ A language which is systematically introduced throughout a country or region, usually by the government.

f) ☐ A language which is convenient when speakers of different languages need to communicate; usually with a limited vocabulary and grammatical structure.

g) ☐ A variety of the language which has the highest status in a nation, usually based on the speech and writing of educated native speakers of the language.

h) ☐ This usually refers to the language that a user feels most comfortable with. It is normally acquired at home or through the influence of, for example, school.

i) ☐ A newly invented word or phrase in a particular language.

j) ☐ A language spoken by relatively few people, for example, in one country or because the numbers of speakers anywhere is relatively small.

Task 4: Predicting content to help understanding

You will notice that Text 7-1 does not have a list of contents. In Ex 4.2, your teacher will show you how to devise a list of your own in the form of questions on the text.

4.1 **Reread Paragraphs A–C of Text 7-1. From reading these paragraphs, what do you think the rest of the article will be about? Write your predictions below.**

_____

_____

_____

_____

_____

_____

_____

_____

_____

4.2 **Think of questions you would like Text 7-1 to answer in relation to the assignment. Base your questions on reading Paragraphs A–C and the background information on Zambia.**

This exercise will serve as an outline of the text and help you read more efficiently.

Example: Why has English become such an influential language in a country like Zambia?

Make a list of similar questions based on your reading of Paragraphs A–C and on the background information on Zambia (page 68 of the Course Book).
Check your answers with other students and with the teacher.

QUESTIONS ABOUT THE TEXT

Why has English become a global language?

_____

_____

_____

_____

_____

_____

Task 5: Selecting relevant information from the text

You should now be ready to carry out the main reading task. You have made decisions about how to read the article and what information you hope to learn from it.

5.1 **Read the rest of Text 7-1 using the following framework.**

- Begin reading the article in the way you have decided is most appropriate.

- Collect relevant information by making notes in the way you think will be most useful.

- Your teacher will give you a time limit for reading and collecting the relevant information. At the end of the time limit, form groups and compare the notes you have made so far.

- Check the information you have agreed on with the teacher.

- Continue reading and making and comparing notes until you have finished the text.

Task 6: Fulfilling your reading purpose

6.1 Using the notes you have made on Text 7-1, write two or three paragraphs in answer to the Focus task.

_____

_____

_____

_____

_____

_____

_____

_____

_____

_____

_____

_____

_____

_____

_____

_____

_____

_____

_____

_____

_____

Unit summary

In this unit you have practised making use of a specific text to support your ideas in a writing assignment, and learnt how knowing subject-specific vocabulary will help you understand texts that you read. You have also developed all the skills you have learnt so far on this reading course.

1   **Look at the topics and lists of subject-specific vocabulary. How quickly can you delete the one word or phrase that does not relate to the topic?**

a)   further education   lectures / assignment / nursery / tutorials / graduation

b)   computers   spreadsheet / virus / template / database / turntable

c)   space exploration   satellite / archaeologist / astronaut / shuttle / orbit

d)   politics   democracy / dictator / free election / divorce / coalition

e)   war and peace   pension / dispute / weapons / troops / ceasefire

2   **Write three topics for which you think you have a good working vocabulary.**

_____   _____   _____

3   **Think about which strategies have helped you improve your reading skills the most. Give one piece of advice about each of the following to a student who is starting the reading course.**

a)   Before reading a text, you should _____

_____

b)   As you read a text, you should _____

_____

c)   After reading a text, you should _____

_____

For web resources relevant to this unit, see:

www.englishforacademicstudy.com/student/reading/links

This weblink will provide additional information about the future of English.

Glossary

Active vocabulary
Vocabulary that you use in your day-to-day life in order to communicate effectively.

Anecdote
A short account of an incident that is amusing or interesting.

Annotate
To write comments or explanatory notes directly onto a text, e.g., in the margin.

Browsing
Reading with no particular aim in mind, e.g., glancing over several pages and checking a few sentences or a heading, or randomly opening a book at a page to read a few lines or paragraphs as a taster.

Collocation
The way that certain words are habitually used together, e.g., *strong cheese* and *fish and chips* collocate, but not *weak cheese* or *chips and fish*.

Complex sentences
Sentences that are made up of several clauses (main and dependent clauses). They may also include long phrases or unusual syntax and/or terminology.

Critical reading
Reading in a way that involves questioning what the text says, what the writer is trying to do and how he or she does this, e.g., whether the text is biased or prejudiced.

Extra-textual information
Information outside the text, such as the 'blurb' on a book cover, diagrams, etc. that help the reader understand what the text is about.

Foreword
A section of a book or longer text that comes at the beginning and gives a short introduction to it. This introduction is often written by someone other than the author and may be in the form of a short essay.

Global summary
A short general summary (usually of one paragraph) that gives the reader a good idea of all the main ideas in a text rather than focusing on any detail. An abstract is one example of a global summary.

Global understanding
This is an understanding of the main idea(s) or argument of a text or conversation. We often skim read (or listen) for global understanding without focusing too much on detail.

Infer
To obtain or work out meaning from the text that the writer has not explicitly stated. This is sometimes called 'reading between the lines' and involves the reader making use of their world knowledge.

Lexical item
An item of vocabulary such as a word or group of words that carry a single meaning, e.g., the word *sure* is one lexical item and *absolutely convinced* is another.

Overt information
Information that is displayed in and around a text, such as headings and titles, text boxes, tables, graphs and diagrams. Overt information, also known as displayed information, often highlights key words and ideas.

Paragraph leader
The first sentence in a written paragraph. The paragraph leader links to the ideas in the previous paragraph and may lead into the ideas in the next paragraph. The paragraph leader can sometimes also be a topic sentence.

Paraphrasing
Explaining or describing the contents or ideas of a text or part of a text, orally or in written form, using your own words and providing your own interpretation.

Prediction
The skill of using what you already know and what you want to know about a topic to guess what the text will contain. Clues such as titles, pictures, layout and paragraph leaders can help you predict and make it less challenging to read or difficult to understand.

Previewing
Looking at text to decide how useful it is for a particular purpose. Previewing might involve looking at: the contents page, the foreword or introduction and/or the index.

Prior knowledge
This is knowledge that you already have about something, sometimes known as *general knowledge* or *world knowledge*. If you have prior knowledge of key vocabulary or ideas in a text, e.g., from reading about it in your own language, you will generally find it easier to follow.

Purposeful reading
Having a specific reason for reading a text, e.g., reading to learn, reading for entertainment or reading to confirm. The reading purpose will affect which reading strategy to apply, e.g., fast skimming, browsing, search reading, intensive reading, etc.

Quoting
Using the exact words of the original text for a specific purpose, orally or in writing.

Reading selectively
Selective reading involves choosing certain sections in a text to read carefully because these are the areas that you wish to understand or research in more depth. You read selectively when you have a clear purpose for reading.

Reading strategy
Something that you can actively do to help your reading, or improve your reading skills over a period of time. Typical reading strategies for academic texts include: knowing your reading purpose, picking out key words and note-taking.

Referencing
Acknowledgement of the sources of ideas and information used or mentioned in a text. References allow a reader to check those sources for accuracy or find out more information about the topic.

Scanning
Reading for specific information involves scanning. It involves finding key words or figures. For example, it is normal to scan a text to find dates, names and specific facts.

Search reading
Looking through a text quickly to find specific *ideas* rather than *words*. It is different from scanning because you do not know the specific words you are looking for.

Skimming
Reading for the general idea or gist of a text involves skimming. It involves reading the text quickly to get the main idea of what it is about rather than focusing on every word. For example, it is normal to skim a letter or book cover to find out what it is about. It often precedes reading for more specific information.

Supporting sentences

Sentences that follow or support the main idea or topic sentence in a paragraph. Supporting sentences may give examples, explanations or additional information about the key idea.

Text analysis

Checking the currency, authorship, purpose, accessibility, relevance and interest value of a text.

Topic sentence

A sentence that carries the main idea of the paragraph. It often comes at the beginning or end of a paragraph, but may also appear elsewhere. It is usually followed by supporting sentences or preceded by them. There may be more than one topic sentence in a paragraph or none at all.

Word class

Words can be grouped into classes according to their function in a sentence. Word classes, also known as parts of speech, include *nouns*, *verbs*, *adjectives* and *adverbs*.

Word family

A group of words that are closely related to each other because they share a common root or because they have related meanings, e.g., *family*, *familiar*, *familiarize*, *familiarization*.